Th

Days

By E W Bullinger

ISBN: 978-1-78364-554-1

www.obt.org.uk

Unless indicated otherwise Scripture quotations are from The Authorized (King James) Version. Rights in the Authorized Version in the United Kingdom are vested in the Crown. Reproduced by permission of the Crown's patentee, Cambridge University Press.

****

THE OPEN BIBLE TRUST
Fordland Mount, Upper Basildon,
Reading, RG8 8LU, UK

THE FOUR DAYS

CONTENTS

INTRODUCTION

INTRODUCTION

In the second Epistle of Paul to Timothy, the Church is seen in its *ruin* (as to its outward manifestation on earth), whereas in the *first* Epistle it is seen in its *rule*. In each of these two spheres the child of God is instructed how to carry himself.

In the *first*, the appointment and qualifications for offices and officers of the Church are dealt with.

In the *second*, all are seen to have failed, and the faithful witness is shown how he is to deal with those who "turn away" from the truth, "err concerning the truth," and who "resist the truth"; and to wait and look for the appearing of "the righteous Judge."

In 2 Tim. 2 there are seven characters in which Timothy, the "man of God," is viewed, and each has its own exhortation.

- In verse 1 he is the "*Son*" and is to "be strong in the grace that is in Christ Jesus."
- In verse 3 he is the "*Soldier,*" and to be "good" he must endure hardness," and not entangle himself "with the affairs of this life, that he may please Him who hath chosen him to be a soldier."
- In verse 5 he is the "*Wrestler,*" and must "strive lawfully."
- In verse 6 he is the "*Husbandman,*" that first partaketh of the fruits.
- In verse 21 he is the *Vessel*," and must be cleansed that he may be "prepared unto every good work"; for only those works are "good" which are prepared works, wrought by a prepared people. All others are either "dead" or "wicked."

- In verse 24 he is the *"Servant of the Lord,"* and must be "gentle . . . apt to teach, patient, in meekness, instructing those that oppose themselves."
- In verse 15 he is the *"Workman"*; and I take this last, and out of its order, because it introduces us to the subject we have in hand.

God's *"workman"* has one aim, and that is to show himself "approved unto God": this is to be his "study": and his work is to be wholly taken up with "the word of truth." Because it is *"truth"* he is to "rightly divide" it.

(1) He is to "divide" its peoples, "Jew, Gentile, and the Church of God" (1 Cor. 10:32). He is not to rob the promises from the Jew and give them to the Church, or to take the privileges of the Church and betray them to the world.

(2) He is to "divide" between *Law* that demands a human righteousness, and *Grace* that bestows a divine righteousness.

(3) He is to "divide" between the two natures: the new nature which cannot sin, and the old nature which cannot but sin.

(4) Between the *Standing* of the Christian in Christ, and his actual life and walk.

(5) Between the *Resurrection, Judgment,* and *Advent* scenes; and lastly,

(6) Between the *Dispensations.*

These dispensations, times, and seasons are clearly distinguished in the Word of God, and our work is *"rightly to divide"* them. God has given a name to each, and we must believe that He means what He says, when, in His "Word of Truth," He speaks of four days, and calls them respectively, "man's day," "the day of Christ," "the day of the Lord," and "the day of God."

These are not meaningless expressions. Each marks a separate and distinct period of time. Each has a morning and an evening, and its own definite duration. Let us first notice …

MAN'S DAY

MAN'S DAY

We read of it in 1 Cor. 4:2. "With me," says the Apostle, "it is a very small matter that I should be judged of you or of man's judgment." In the margin you find that the word judgment is in the Greek, "*day*"; man's day – *i.e.*, the word judgment is in the Greek, "*day; man's day*" – *i.e.*, the day when man is judging, as distinguished from the day when the Lord will judge. To this he refers in verse 6, when he adds,

> "Therefore judge nothing before the time until the Lord come."

Man's day had a morning; it is not necessary for us to definitely set a date for its evening, but it is sufficient for us to know that it is the day in which we are living, the day which is fast running on to its evening, and which will end when the next day, "the day of Christ," shall dawn.

"Man's day," like all the others, is marked by its own peculiar characteristics. It is marked by the absence of Christ, and by the presence of the Holy Ghost: and this reminds us that while it is in one sense the day when man is working, it is in another sense the dispensation of the Holy Spirit, in which He is working, and taking out from among men a people whom He is making ready for the Lord and, like Eleazer of old, is revealing to many a heart the tokens of the wealth of the Father, and the love of the Son, and leading home the bride to the true Isaac, who in the "eventide" will come forth into the air to meet and to greet her, and receive her to Himself.

But the great mark of "man's day" is that man is speaking and God is silent; man is having his say and God is holding His peace. In other days and dispensations God has spoken "at sundry times and in divers manners." He last spoke by His Son, and when man murdered that Blessed One, God left man to himself to manifest on the one hand the world's foolishness and His people's faithfulness.

From that moment man has been manifesting his folly:

> "The godly ceaseth; the faithful fail from among the children of man. They speak vanity every one with his neighbor: with flattering lips and with a double heart do they speak" (Psa. 12:1, 2).

Man talks of regenerating the world; he puts forth his plans and remedies for the evils which he would fain remove. He talks of science and commerce, education and reforms, by which he promises to empty our prisons and workhouses; but, alas! He fails to see that no moral reforms can ever remove the curse from the earth, nor perform those physical marvels which alone can give them that which he ignorantly strives after. Poor man! He has had full scope: ample time to test his schemes.

As to good *government*, he seems as far from it as ever; as to his religion, it only tends to increase the thralldom in which he lives. His folly is well-nigh perfected; his impotence is well nigh manifested. "He that sitteth in the Heavens" is silent, but He *laughs*. The Lord has them in derision, and when He speaks to them it will be "in his wrath," to "vex them in his sore displeasure."

But God's silence also tests His people's *faithfulness*. The last words of the Son were, "Ye shall be witnesses unto me." God's people now – during "man's day" – occupy the position of the prophets of old. The Hebrew word *Nabi* means one who speaks for another. This is the meaning of the Greek equivalent, *prophetes,* which we spell with English letters *prophet.* When God said to Moses (Ex. 7:1), "Aaron shall be thy prophet," He meant, as it is rendered in Ex. 4:1, "Aaron shall be thy *spokesman.*"

Now it is clear that to speak for another requires special qualification. The spokesman must be informed of what he is to say. Hence the prophet was one who was always qualified by *God's Spirit* (Num. 11:29; 12:6). Hence Nehemiah says (9:30),

> "Many years didst thou forbear them, and testifiedst against them *by thy Spirit in thy prophets.*"

And it is said of Haggai (1:13),

> "Then spake Haggai, the Lord's messenger, in the Lord's message."

To enable His people now to be His spokesmen, God qualifies them by the same means – by His Spirit, and also by His Word. It is only by acquaintance with God's Word that we can know what we are to speak. Hence the command to Ezekiel was (3:17),

> "Hear the word at my mouth and give them warning from Me." This is why in the Old Testament the prophet was called a *"man of God."*

Ezekiel, the man who belongs to God, who was sent by God, and qualified by God. That is why the term in the New Testament is confined to the one who learns, and is assured of, and is made wise by the word of God.

> "All scripture is given by inspiration of God, and is profitable for doctrine, for reproof, for correction, for instruction in righteousness: that the MAN OF GOD may be perfect, thoroughly furnished unto all good works." (2 Tim. 3:16, 17)

Or, according to the Greek, furnished, thoroughly furnished; or perfect, thoroughly perfected; or fitted, thoroughly fitted unto all good works. Only such an one is a "Man of God," and only such an one is qualified to speak for God and to witness for Him in this day of His silence.

This is the position of God's people now; and this is their power for service. When Paul was converted and sent forth, his commission ran,

> "Thou shalt be His *witness*" (Acts 22:15),

and again,

> "I have appeared unto thee for this purpose, to make thee a minister and *a witness* (Acts 26:16).

Peter confessed that he was "an elder and *a witness*" (1 Pet. 5:16), and Jesus said,

> "For this cause came I into the world, that I should *bear witness of the Truth*" (John 18:37).

He was *"**the** faithful witness."*

The witnessing *for* God was always, and will necessarily always be, *against* man, simply because man's thoughts and man's ways are opposite to God's (Isa. 55:8). Thus we read, when Jeremiah was commissioned, Jehovah said unto him,

> "Thou therefore gird up thy loins, and arise, and speak unto them all that I command thee: be not dismayed at their faces, lest I confound thee before them. For, behold, I have made thee this day a defenced city, and an iron pillar, and brazen walls against the whole land, against the kings of Judah, against the princes thereof, against the priests thereof, and against the people of the land. And they shall fight against thee; but they shall not prevail against thee; for I am with thee; saith the Lord, to deliver thee" (Jer. 1:17-19).

From this we learn than if we witness *for* God, it must be also *"against"* man, and his words, his maxims, and his ways. God's prophets were men who could never swim with the stream, they were never popular, they could never make popularity their aim, they could never look on success as their end. And it is the same today with God's spokesmen and witnesses.

> "Yea, and all that will (*i.e. are determined to*) live godly (*i.e., like God*) in Christ Jesus shall suffer persecution" (2 Tim. 3:15).

If any of you do not believe it, try it! Be a faithful witness for God; dare to stand alone with Him, and you will soon see that you will have to "suffer persecution."

All witness-bearing now is defined in Rev. 19:10, where we read, "The testimony of Jesus is the spirit of prophecy"; that is to say, the spirit of all true speaking for God is testimony concerning Jesus.

God's *silence* thus defines the office and duty of all his children. Hence, while they are called "Christians" only three times in the New Testament, and "Churchmen" never, they are spoken of as *witnesses* upwards of *eighty* times. The one word which describes them more accurately than any other is the one word that man does not regard as "respectable," and that is "PROTESTANT!"

A true Protestant is one who bears testimony for (*"pro"*) God and His truth against man and his vanities. This name is more ancient than the Reformation, for Jerome (in the Latin Vulgate) speaks of Jehovah sending His ...

> "prophets to them, to bring them again unto the Lord; and they *testified* against them: but they would not hear" (2 Chron. 24:19).

The word rendered "and they testified," stand in the Latin *"quos protestants,"* *i.e.,* who witnessed for God, and against men, or literally *who were Protestants.* Oh, let us not be ashamed of the word which so well sets forth our high and holy calling, but let us exalt it and honour it; and though man may dislike it and cast us out, we may be content to be unpopular, counting it all joy to suffer shame for His name.

Man's day is drawing to its close. It is indeed called "day" only from man's point of view. It is not really "day." God calls it "night," and, thank God, the same word that tells us it is night, tells us also that "it is far spent," and that the day – the *true* day – is at hand.

It will end as the former dispensation ended – in darkness and stout words against the Lord. But we learn that it is possible to walk with Him in the darkest days; for Enoch walked with God 365 years before the judgment of the Flood. While Jehovah had to say of man in the dark days before Christ's *first* coming, "Your words have been stout against me," yet, of His people it is written:

> "THEN they that feared the Lord spake often one to another: and the Lord hearkened and heard it, and a book of remembrance was written before Him for them that feared the Lord, and that thought upon His name" (Mal. 3:13, 16)

Oh! what wonderful silence! How eloquent! What marvellous patience! What wondrous long-suffering! Oh! Listen to this silence of God! It tells of one other thing. Besides manifesting man's *folly* and His people's *faithfulness*, it tells also of His grace. The Lord waits that He may be gracious.

"The long-suffering of our Lord is salvation" (2 Pet. 3:15).

He waits to "accomplish the number of the elect." And when this is complete, then once again He will speak, and His first word will end "man's day," and usher in …

THE DAY OF CHRIST

THE DAY OF CHRIST

This is no mere theory. God has given us and written down the very words that He will utter, in the fiftieth Psalm. A moment is coming (oh, that it were here!) when it will be said,

> "The mighty God even the Lord, hath spoken, and called the earth from the rising of the sun unto the going down thereof. Out of Zion, the perfection of beauty, God hath shined." (*vv.* 1, 2)

Yes!

> "Our God shall come, and shall not keep silence" (*v.* 3).

> "He shall call to the heavens from above, and to the earth, that He may judge His people." (*v.* 4)

He will speak to His *Saints*, and His first words will be, "GATHER MY SAINTS TOGETHER UNTO ME." Some of His saints stand now, like John, in Rev. 4:1, waiting to see the door opened in Heaven, and to hear His voice say, "Come up hither." They wait to hear "the shout" of 1 Thess. 4:16 – the assembling shout. For this shout is no mere inarticulate noise. The peculiar word used shows it to be the *gathering* shout, the shout that will gather His saints together unto Himself for unto Him shall "the gathering of the people be."

When we shall be thus gathered "to meet the Lord in the air," that will be for us "the day of Christ." "*Christ*" means "*the anointed one.*" It is used of Jesus as glorified and exalted, "for God hath made this same Jesus both Lord and Christ."

"The day of Christ" is the time during which His saints are with Him in the Heavenlies, before their return with Him in glorious majesty to the Earth. It begins with his coming FOR His saints, and it will end with His coming WITH them.

We must dismiss from our minds the idea that Christ's coming consists of one single act of a momentary duration[1]. His *second* coming will be, in a very important manner, like His *first* coming. His *first* coming consisted of many events spread over a number of years, and each event went to make up that *first* coming.

For example, a Jew would read in Micah 5:2,

> "But thou Bethlehem Ephratah, though thou be little among the thousands of Judah, yet out of thee SHALL HE COME FORTH unto Me that is to be ruler in Israel," etc.

But he also read, in Zech. 9:19,

> "Rejoice greatly, O daughter of Sion; shout, O daughter of Jerusalem: behold, Thy king COMETH UNTO thee."

There was nothing to tell him that THIRTY-THREE YEARS were to elapse between those two events, which both speak of His

---

[1] On this, and some other statements in this section, Bullinger was to change his understanding. His mature views can be seen in his last book *The Foundations of Dispensational Truth*, published by The Open Bible Trust. Details are given towards the end of this book.

coming, but we know that such was the case. In like manner, it is only by comparing Scripture with Scripture, that we can know that there will be a definite interval of probably seven years at least, between the "coming forth" spoken of in 1 Thess. 4:16,

> "The Lord Himself shall descend from Heaven with a shout," etc.,

and the "coming unto," 2 Thess. 1:7,

> "When the Lord Jesus shall be revealed from Heaven with His mighty angels, in flaming fire taking vengeance on them that know not God, and that obey not the gospel of our Lord Jesus Christ."

That interval is called "the day of Christ." Many events may take place during that day, but we are told of *two* which will in importance exceed all others:

(1) The trial of the saints' service; and
(2) The marriage of the Lamb.

In the only places where we read of "the day of Christ" it is connected with our service and with work.

> "Being confident of this very thing, that he which hath begun *a good work* in you will perform it until *the day of Christ*." (Phil. 1:6)

This tells us that all our good works are only the *working out* of what God has previously *worked in*.

"Work out your own salvation with fear and trembling. For it is God that worketh in you, both to will and to do of His good pleasure." (Phil. 2:12, 13)

"That ye may approve things that are excellent (or, margin, try things that differ); that ye may be sincere and without offence till *the day of Christ*; being filled with the fruits of righteousness, which are by Jesus Christ, unto the glory and praise of God." (Phil. 1:10,11)

Here, again, that day is connected with our *fruits*, and with our service. Still more clear is …

"Do all things without murmurings and disputings: that ye may be blameless and harmless, the sons of God, without rebuke, in the midst of a crooked and perverse nation, among whom ye shine as lights in the world; holding forth the word of life; that I may rejoice in *the day of Christ*, that I have not run in vain, neither laboured in vain." (Phil. 2:14-16)

The reference here is unmistakable. In that day all running and labouring will be tested, for:

"every man's work shall be made manifest, for the day shall declare it, because it shall be revealed by fire; and the fire shall try every man's work of what work of what sort it is. If any man's work abide which he hath built thereupon, he shall receive a reward. If any man's work shall be burned, he shall suffer loss: but he himself shall be *saved*" (1 Cor. 3:13-15).

This is why we are not to trouble ourselves about "MAN'S DAY," or man's judgment, for the Lord will, in *the day of Christ*,

> "make manifest the counsels of the heart: and then shall every man have praise of God." (1 Cor. 4:5)

All that we have done to get the "praise of man" will be burned up. God will not accept it. Only that which has been done with a single eye for His glory can have His praise. And how little that will be, alas, our own hearts can testify!

It is thus, during *the day of Christ*, that the *Bema* of Christ will be set (2 Cor. 5:10). The *Bema* is not a throne for the judgment and acquittal of criminals, but of *awards* and bestowals of crowns for service. Only His saints will be there, raised in "incorruption," "glory," and "power;" changed and made like His own body of glory before they stand there; perfect in all Christ's perfection; holy in His holiness; righteous in all His righteousness; comely in His comeliness. They will stand there as what He has made them, therefore they "shall not come into judgment" (John 5:24). For them there is "no condemnation" (Rom. 8:1). But for their works, their ministry, their running, their labours – *these* are not all "acceptable" to Him, though *they* [the people] are for ever "accepted in the Beloved."

How long this manifestation will be in its duration we know not, for we are not told; but we do know what will take place when it shall have ended.

Rev. 19 describes the heavenly scene. Great voices are heard. The command goes forth:

"Let us be glad and rejoice, and give honour to Him: for the marriage of the Lamb is come, and His wife hath made herself ready." (Rev. 19:7)

Yes, ready – not by her service down here, but by the *sanctifying* and *cleansing* which she has undergone before the *Bema* of Christ. Himself hath done it,

"that He might present it to Himself a glorious church, not having spot, or wrinkle, or any such thing; but that it should be holy and without blemish" (Eph. 5:26, 27).

The days of her purification in the Heavenlies shall then be ended. All the spots and stains of her unfaithfulness washed out, all her faults, failures, and infirmities cleansed, all her poor services sanctified under the eye of her beloved. Then it will be said, "She hath made herself ready" – and

"to her was granted that she should be arrayed in fine linen, clean and white; for the fine linen is the righteousness of saints. And he saith unto me write, Blessed are they which are called unto the marriage supper of the Lamb." (Rev. 19:8-9)

Then, immediately after this, we read, "And I saw heaven opened" (not a "door," as when they ascended thither, Rev. 4:1), and forth comes He who is "faithful and true" – "the Word of God," and the armies in Heaven follow Him, clothed in pure linen, white and clean.

He comes "to judge and make war" – to "smite the nations" – to "rule them with a rod of iron" – to tread "the wine-press of the fierceness of the wrath of Almighty God."

In Rev. 19:19 verse the battle is set in array. The war commences, and the first act recorded is:

"the beast was taken, and with him the false prophet ... These both were cast alive into a lake of fire burning with brimstone."

What does this tell us? It speaks to us of what has been going on in the earth during the heavenly scene we have been describing.

While it has been *"the day of Christ"* in Heavenlies, it has been the *day of Antichrist* on the earth. And what that will be is beyond our imagination. No tongue can tell how rapid will be the corruption on the earth the moment the salt has been removed. It will outstrip all our present ideas of corruptibility. We see corruption *now* all around us, but it is hindered and checked by the presence of the Holy Ghost in the Church, but when that wicked one shall be revealed ...

"even him, whose coming is after the working of Satan with all power and signs and lying wonders," etc., (2 Thess. 2:7-12).

Then will be the "time of Jacob's trouble, but he shall be saved out of it" (Jer. 30:7). Matt. 24[2] and Rev. 6-18 describe that scene of tribulation. It is not within our purpose now to enlarge upon it. Much is revealed with regard to the Antichrist[3] and "his time,"

---

[2] For more on this chapter see *Signs of the Second Coming: Matthew 24* by Michael Penny, published by The Open Bible Trust.

[3] For more on this see *The Mark of the Beast and the Jerusalem Temple*, by Michael Penny, published by The Open Bible Trust.

and those who desire to know all that God has revealed, have only to study what he has written concerning it.

One question demands a reply, and that is the oft-repeated one, "Will the Church be in the tribulation?" The answer is clear, what are we to understand by the term "the Church"? Is it the whole body of professors? Then certainly the answer is, Yes! A part of *such* a church will of necessity be left behind when the Lord descends into the air to gather his saints[4].

But if by "the Church" is meant the "Body" of Christ, then we answer, NO!

The order of resurrection is declared:

"Christ the first fruits, afterward they that are Christ's at His coming." (1 Cor. 15:23)

Thus the point is settled. For how do we become "Christ's"? Surely it is by birth; not by behaviour. Surely it is a question of *life*, and not of *light*.

To err here is to be ignorant as to the very first principles of *salvation by grace*. Those who are "Christ's" have been quickened from their death in sin, by the Holy Ghost, to a new, spiritual, and eternal life. They are made members of His Body, righteous, holy, and perfect *in Him*. If they are *"in Christ"* now, they will be *"in Christ"* and *"with Christ"* at His coming.

He is coming to receive them to Himself, and how can the trial of their service take place; and how can they be "called to the

---

[4] For a detailed discussion of this see *The Great Tribulation* by William Campbell, published by The Open Bible Trust.

marriage supper of the Lamb" while any of them are down here suffering under Antichrist? The thought is monstrous; and any Scriptures that may seem to imply it must be explained on some other grounds than those which would destroy the very essence of the great and glorious truth of "Salvation by grace alone."

True, there will be "a great multitude" saved during, in, and through that great tribulation. This we learn from Rev. 7:9. And Isaiah says,

> "When thy judgments are in the earth, the inhabitants of the world will learn righteousness." (Isa, 26:9)

But to be "saved" is not necessarily to form part of "the Church," or "the Body of Christ." There are "the nations of them which are saved" (Rev. 21:24). And one "star differeth from star in glory."

So it is possible for a multitude to be saved through that great tribulation, so great that "no man could number it," and yet for that great multitude to occupy its own position. And so it will be.

- *"They stand* before the throne."
  - But the Church will *sit* upon His throne.
- They "serve God day and night in His temple."
  - But the Church will reign with Christ.
- "The Lamb which is in the midst of the throne shall ... *lead* them."
  - But the "Church" will not thus be led, but will be "with Christ *where He is*," and be the *leader* rather than a *follower*.

In this, as in all other subjects, our differences will be lessened in proportion as we are able accurately to define our terms.

But now we come to the third day.

THE LORD'S DAY

THE LORD'S DAY

This will commence with the coming forth of the Lord Jesus, with all His saints, to destroy the Antichrist and all His enemies, and to take unto Himself His great power, and reign.

It is the day when the Lord will judge, and interfere once more directly in the course of this world's politics. So that, in one sense, it may be said to commence with the first issuing forth of the premonitory judgments in the earth – even while "the day of Christ" is yet running and finishing its course "in the air." But its dawning will be with the actual bursting forth of "the Sun of righteousness" with healing in His wings for His people Israel.

And here we must consider an instructive passage, 2 Thess. 2:1, 2, for at first sight it not only presents a difficulty but is in itself unintelligible as it stands in the Authorised Version. We will give it, therefore, from the Revised Version.

> "Now we beseech you, brethren, touching the coming of our Lord Jesus Christ, and our gathering together unto Him; to the end that ye be not quickly shaken from your mind, nor yet be troubled, either by spirit, or by word, or by epistle, as from us, as that the day of the Lord is now present."

This is the correct rendering: for

(1) The term "day of the Lord" is based on the authority of the three great ancient MSS., and it is the reading in every *critical* Greek text that has ever been published;

(2) The word translated "at hand" means literally: "*has set in*," or is now present.

It occurs seven times, and is so translated – *e.g.*

- Rom. 8:30, "things *present*;
- Gal 1:4, "*this present* evil world";
- 1 Cor. 3:22, "things *present*";
- 1 Cor. 7:26, "this is good for the *present* distress";
- Heb. 9:9, the tabernacle was "a figure for the time then *present*";
- 2 Tim. 3:1, "in the last days perilous times shall come," *i.e., be present.*

This is every place where the Greek word translated "at hand" occurs. Again, the English term "at hand" occurs in nineteen other passages, but in none of these is it the rendering of the Greek word employed in 2 Thess. 2:2.

There was every reason therefore why they, the Thessalonian saints, should be troubled if "the day of the Lord" had set in, because it would have proved that "*the day of Christ*" had come and gone, and they had not been gathered. Thus the meaning of the passage is clear and its lesson is most solemn.

"The day of the Lord" is the day[5] when the Lord will judge or rule: when He will again take the world in hand: when "the loftiness of men shall be bowed down, and the haughtiness of men shall be made low, and the Lord alone shall be exalted in that

---

[5] For more on this see *The Lord's Day (Revelation 1:10)* by E W Bullinger, and *The Day of the Lord! When?* By Michael Penny, both published by The Open Bible Trust. Details given towards the end of this book.

day." It is the day of which the Old Testament Scriptures are full. It will be:

> "a day of darkness and of gloominess, a day of clouds and of thick darkness ... there hath not been ever the like, neither shall be any more after it." (Joel 2:2)

It is the day when "the Lord shall be King over all the earth." When He shall judge the people with righteousness and the poor with judgment. When "all kings shall fall down before Him and all nations shall do Him service." When he shall be "King of kings and Lord of lords," and all the kingdoms of our Lord and of His Christ.

It comes "IMMEDIATELY after the tribulation of those days," when:

> "the sun shall be darkened, and the moon shall not give her light, and the stars shall fall from heaven, and the powers of the heavens shall be shaken: and then shall appear the sign of the Son of Man in the heaven: and then shall all the tribes of the earth mourn, and they shall see the Son of Man coming in the clouds of heaven with power and great glory" (Matt. 24:29, 30).

It lasts for a thousand years. It is not possible for us here to speak of all its wonderful events – of the judgments which usher it in – of the righteousness, joy, and peace which will then fill the earth (as now they are shed abroad in the heart by the Holy Ghost, giving the Lord's people a foretaste of it). One thing, however, we must notice, because it is the key to the book of Revelation.

John became in Spirit on "the Lord's day." We can conceive of no reason why it should be important to record that John had this revelation on any particular day of the week, and it is a gratuitous assumption to suppose that the Lord's day here means our Sunday, or as some have gone so far as to imagine an "Easter Sunday"! Sunday in the New Testament is invariably called "the first day of the week" (Matt. 28:1; Mark 16:2, 9; Luke 24:1; John 20:1, 19; Acts 20:7; 1 Cor. 16:2). It was not called "the Lord's day" until long after this, and then the practice arose from a misunderstanding of Rev. 1:10.

In other words, Sunday was not called "the Lord's day" in Rev. 1:10, because of any prevailing custom, but the custom afterwards obtained through a misapprehension that John so called it in this passage.

It may be objected that the usual designation of "the Lord's day" is by the use of two nouns, the latter being in the genitive case (*e.g.*, "the day of the Lord"), and not by the use of the adjective, as in Rev. 1:10, "the Lord's day." But the objection is groundless in the absence of any proof that the Sunday was already so called in the days of the Evangelist. On the other hand it may be urged:

(1) that by the used of the adjective it is brought into greater and better apposition with "man's day" in 1 Cor. 4:3. "Man's day" is the period during which man is judging and ruling; but "the Lord's day" will be the day when man will be abased and the Lord alone shall be exalted.

(2) But, there is something more in the use of the adjective here. Had the two nouns been used, the emphasis would have been on the word "*Lord*" – *i.e.*, the day belonging to or proceeding from the Lord. With the noun in the genitive

case, the day is lost in the possessor to whom it belongs, the author from whom it proceeds. Whereas, with the adjective, the emphasis is on the word "*day*." It is the *day* that is uppermost in the thought; it is the *day* which is characterized by the Lord's presence and action. This is confirmed by the use of this adjective, in the only other place in which it is used, 1 Cor 11:20, "the Lord's Table." Had the two nouns been employed here (*e.g., the Supper of the Lord*), the emphasis would have been on the origin of that supper, as being instituted and partaken of by the Lord. But it is not so; it is "the Lord's *Supper.*" The emphasis is on the word *"supper,"* and the thought is, that out of all the "suppers" of which we partake, this is the Lord's, this is the one to which He, by His presence in our hearts by faith, gives its peculiar character, and thus distinguishes it from all others.

Hence we conclude that, by the Spirit, John was taken into the future scenes and events of "the Lord's day." He sees them pass before him in vision, and he records them for our instruction. In Rev. 6 – 18, we have the darkness before the dawn – the preliminary judgments (while yet the Church is with the Lord in the air) which will issue in the complete ejection of the usurper from this world. "Judgment" has even now been declared.

"Now is the judgment of this world." (John 12:31)

Sentence has been passed. A judgment-summons has been obtained and presently "execution" will be put in. Those preliminary judgments of the trumpets and vials will be followed by the revelation of the Rightful King from Heaven followed by His armies, and then "the day of the Lord" will run on its blessed and happy course for a thousand years.

As it is impossible for us to imagine the awful rapidity and extent of the evil and the corruption during the day of Antichrist, when the salt – the Church – shall have been removed, so is it impossible for us to imagine the universal blessedness which shall reign and prevail when Satan shall be bound?

> "Oh! what a bright and blessed world,
> This groaning earth of ours will be,
> When from its throne, the Tempter, hurled,
> Shall leave it all, O Lord, to Thee."

But this day, like all that precede it, will have an evening, for at its close Satan "must be loosed a little season." This will be followed by the great apostacy of the nations, but it will be of brief duration. The great white throne will be set. The judgment of the wicked dead will take place, Death and the grave shall be destroyed for ever, and the next day will dawn ...

THE DAY OF GOD

THE DAY OF GOD

Peter speaks of it in 2 Pet. 3:12. "The day of the Lord" will come in like a thief, and have a glorious noon; but it will go out with an awful night. In

> "the coming of THE DAY OF GOD ... the heavens being on fire shall be dissolved, and the elements shall melt with fervent heat. Nevertheless we, according to His promise, look for new heavens and a new earth, wherein dwelleth righteousness" (2 Pet. 3:12, 13).

Immediately after the final judgment, John says (Rev. 21:1),

> "And I saw a new heaven and a new earth: for the first (or former) heaven and the first earth were passed away."

The Holy Spirit tells us by Peter *how* they shall pass away; and by Paul He tells us that when

> "the last enemy shall have been destroyed,"

and

> "all things subdued unto Him, then shall the Son also Himself be subject unto Him that put all things under Him, that GOD MAY BE ALL IN ALL." (1 Cor. 15:25-28)

This will be "the day of God," when God shall be all in all. This shall be "a morning without clouds," a day that shall have no evening, and know no night. "There shall be no night there" (Rev. 21:25).

There is very little revealed to us concerning this day. The full knowledge of it must be reserved till we shall be there. And oh! What it will be to be there!

> "We speak of the realms of the blest,
> That country so bright and so fair,
> And oft are its glories confessed,
> But what will it be to be there!"

Oh! To be there!

This is the one great commanding thought now, that overtops all other considerations. No other subject can approach it in importance. All others are vanity itself in comparison to it.

May the Lord use this outline of these solemn truths to awaken any who are careless or indifferent to these eternal realities; and stir us all up to holy living, and a deeper interest in their study.

This is the concluding lesson drawn from a consideration of these things, by the Spirit of God Himself.

> "Seeing then that all these things shall be dissolved what manner of persons ought ye to be in all holy conversation and godliness; looking for and hasting unto the coming day of God, wherein the heavens being on fire shall be dissolved, and the elements shall melt with fervent heat? Nevertheless we, according to His promise, look for new heavens and a new earth, wherein dwelleth righteousness. Wherefore, beloved, seeing that ye look for such things, be diligent that ye may be found of Him in peace, without spot, and blameless. And account that the long-suffering of our Lord is salvation." (2 Pet. 3:11-15)

****

ALSO ON THIS SUBJECT

ALSO ON THIS SUBJECT

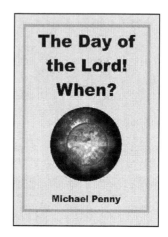

The Lord's Day
(Revelation 1:10)
By E W Bullinger

The Lord's Day! Is it Saturday? Or Sunday? Or is it "The Great and Terrible Day of the Lord" spoken of by the Prophets?

These are important questions, for this expression opens Revelation and how we understand this expression will determine where in time we place the action described in the rest of Revelation and will, in some ways, affect our interpretation of the whole book.

This publication contains *all* that Bullinger has written on *The Lord's Day* and Revelation 1:10. It has combined his writings on the subject from his magazine *Things to Come* and from his books *How to Enjoy the Bible* and *The Apocalypse* (later editions entitled *Commentary on Revelation*).

We hope the reader will study this book and appreciate why Bullinger's scholarship and attention to detail is still valued by many today.

****

The Day of the Lord!
When?
By Michael Penny

Joel wrote about *the great and dreadful day of the Lord*. And Amos told us that it was a day of darkness, not light, when it would be pitch-dark without a ray of brightness. He goes on to say that it will be as though a man fled from a lion only to meet a bear; as though a man entered his house and rested his hand on the wall only to have a snake bite him.

- Has this *great and dreadful day of the Lord* already taken place or is it still future?
- And is there more than one *day of the Lord*?

These are just two of the issues the author considers in this publication which will help many Christians gain a better understanding of what the biblical writers meant by *The Day of the Lord.*

ABOUT THE AUTHOR

Ethelbert W. Bullinger D.D. (1837-1913) was a direct descendant of Heinrich Bullinger, the great Swiss reformer who carried on Zwingli's work after the latter had been killed in war.

E. W. Bullinger was brought up a Methodist but sang in the choir of Canterbury Cathedral in Kent. He trained for and became an Anglican (Episcopalian) minister before becoming Secretary of the Trinitarian Bible Society. He was a man of intense spirituality and made a number of outstanding contributions to biblical scholarship and broad-based evangelical Christianity.

BULLINGER'S LAST BOOK

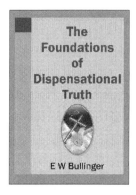

The
Foundations
of
Dispensational
Truth

E W Bullinger

The Foundations of Dispensational Truth

Bullinger's last book,
reflecting his mature views.

This is Bullinger's last book and is his definitive work on the subject of dispensationalism. It covers the ministries of ...

- the prophets,
- the Son of God,
- those that heard Christ, and
- the ministry of Paul, the Apostle to the Gentiles.

He comments on the Gospels and the Pauline epistles and has a lengthy section on the Acts of the Apostles, followed by one explaining why miraculous signs of the Acts period ceased.

This is a newly typeset book, well presented in an easy to read format.

Copies of *The Foundations of Dispensational Truth,*
and of the books listed on the previous pages
and next pages,
are available from

www.obt.org.uk

and from

The Open Bible Trust,
Fordland Mount, Upper Basildon,
Reading, RG8 8LU, UK.

They also available as eBooks
from Amazon Kindle and Apple,
and as KDP paperbacks from Amazon.

The following is a selection of works by E W Bullinger published by The Open Bible Trust

The Transfiguration
The Knowledge of God
God's Purpose in Israel
The Prayers of Ephesians
The Lord's Day (Revelation 1:10)
The Rich Man and Lazarus
The Importance of Accuracy
Christ's Prophetic Teaching
The Resurrection of the Body
The Divine Names and Titles
The Spirits in Prison: 1 Peter 3:17-4:6
The Lesson of the Book of Job: The Oldest Lesson in the World
The Seven Sayings to the Woman at the Well
The Foundations of Dispensational Truth
The Christian's Greatest Need
Introducing the Church Epistles
The Two Natures in the Child of God
The Name of Jehovah in the Book of Esther
The Names and Order of the Books of the Old Testament
The Second Advent in Relation to the Jew
The Vision of Isaiah: Its Structure and Scope
The Importance of Accuracy: in the study of the Bible

More information about the above can be seen on www.obt.org.uk from where they can be ordered.

FURTHER READING

The Development of Dispensationalism
By Michael Penny

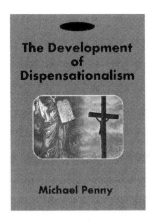

This book starts off by considering the theology of four of the earliest church fathers:

- Justin Martyr (110-165)
- Irenaeus (130-200)
- Clement of Alexandria (150-220)
- Augustine (354-430)

The author then contrasts their approach to the Bible (which could be termed embryonic dispensationalism) with that of such people as Tertullian (155-222) and Origen (185-254), whose approach was to spiritualize or allegorize.

The healthy debate between two such approaches was cut short by Constantine and the Catholic Church which favoured allegorizing. That was until the reformation when people turned back to the Bible and began to read it and understand it in a more literal way. As a result, Christians, such as Miles Coverdale, began to realise that God had spoken

- at different times.
- to different people,
- in different ways,

This is the basis of a dispensational approach and the author does an excellent job is showing how this approach has developed since the Reformation and into the 21st Century.

Search magazine

For a free sample of
the Open Bible Trust's magazine Search,
please email

admin@obt.org.uk

or visit

www.obt.org.uk/search

ABOUT THIS BOOK

The Four Days

The times and seasons and dispensations are clearly distinguished in the Word of God, and the work of the student of the Bible is to "*rightly to divide*" them.

God has given a name to each, and we must believe that He means what He says, when, in His "Word of Truth," He speaks of four days, and calls them respectively,

- Man's Day,
- The Day of Christ,
- The Day of the Lord, and
- The Day of God.

These are not meaningless expressions. Each marks a separate and distinct period of time. Each has a morning and an evening, and its own definite duration.

Publications of The Open Bible Trust must be in accordance with its evangelical, fundamental and dispensational basis. However, beyond this minimum, writers are free to express whatever beliefs they may have as their own understanding, provided that the aim in so doing is to further the object of The Open Bible Trust. A copy of the doctrinal basis is available on **www.obt.org.uk** or from:

THE OPEN BIBLE TRUST
Fordland Mount, Upper Basildon,
Reading, RG8 8LU, UK

Made in the USA
Columbia, SC
08 July 2025

60486142R20035